SAMURAI

GAIL TERP

BLACK
RABBIT
BOOKS

Bolt is published by Black Rabbit Books
P.O. Box 3263, Mankato, Minnesota, 56002.
www.blackrabbitbooks.com
Copyright © 2020 Black Rabbit Books

Marysa Storm, editor; Grant Gould, designer;
Omay Ayres, photo researcher

Names: Terp, Gail, 1951-
Title: Samurai / by Gail Terp.
Description: Mankato, Minnesota : Black Rabbit Books, 2020. | Series:
Bolt. History's warriors | Includes bibliographical references and index.
Identifiers: LCCN 2018011272 (print) | LCCN 2018012096 (ebook) |
ISBN 9781680728590 (e-book) | ISBN 9781680728538 (library binding) |
ISBN 9781644660447 (paperback)
Subjects: LCSH: Samurai–Juvenile literature.
Classification: LCC DS827.S3 (ebook) | LCC DS827.S3 T47 2020 (print) |
DDC 952/.025–dc23
LC record available at https://lccn.loc.gov/2018011272

Printed in the United States. 1/19

CONTENTS

CHAPTER 1

Meet the SAMURAI

In 1612, two samurai agreed to fight. They wanted to find out who was the better swordsman. Kojiro arrived on time. But his **opponent** didn't. Hours late, Musashi arrived by boat. He had a long wooden sword. He carved it from an oar on his way. Kojiro was angry. No one made him wait!

Duel to the Death

Finally, the fight began. Angry, Kojiro attacked first. Musashi struck back. He swung his wooden sword at Kojiro's side. The force broke his ribs. One rib cut Kojiro's lung, and he died. Musashi won. But he felt no success. The great Kojiro would never fight again.

Musashi arrived late on purpose. He knew it'd make Kojiro mad.

Ancient Japan

Samurai were highly skilled warriors in **ancient** Japan. They fought against invaders and other samurai. For a while, ninja existed at the same time as samurai. Ninja were used for spying and other secretive missions.

Samurai served wealthy leaders called daimyos. In return, they gave samurai power and land.

World of the Samurai

SAMURAI IN ANCIENT JAPAN

Samurai lived in a class system. They were part of the ruling class.

EMPEROR

ROYAL CLASS

shogun

daimyos

RULING CLASS

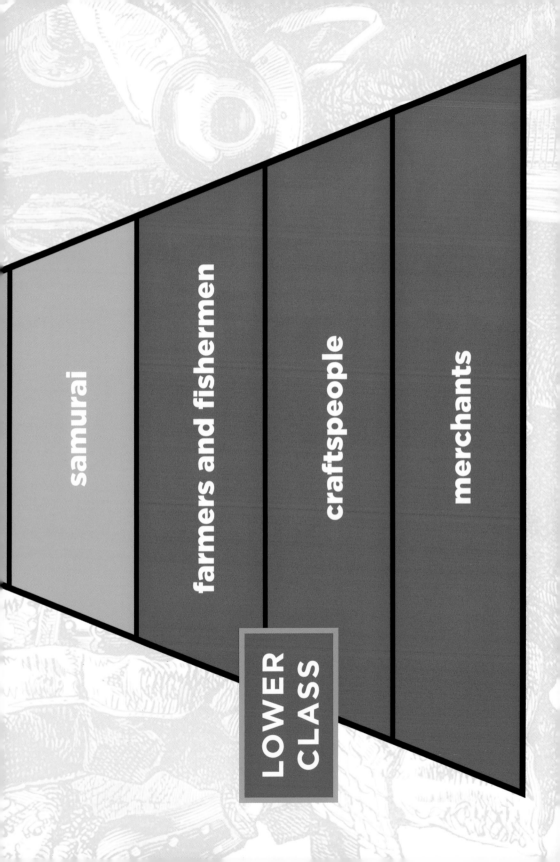

samurai

farmers and fishermen

craftspeople

merchants

LOWER CLASS

The word samurai
means "those who serve"
in Japanese.

CHAPTER 2

Samurai

When not fighting, samurai oversaw workers on their land. They also had families. Children of samurai became warriors too. They started training by age five. Some trained at home. They learned from their fathers or uncles. Others went to schools. They practiced fighting with and without weapons.

Girls trained as samurai too. Many didn't fight on the battlefield. But they were expected to protect their homes.

Samurai Training

Samurai also trained in the arts. They studied poetry. They practiced painting. These activities required focus. They taught warriors to be calm. Being calm allowed warriors to concentrate. It led to stronger fighting skills.

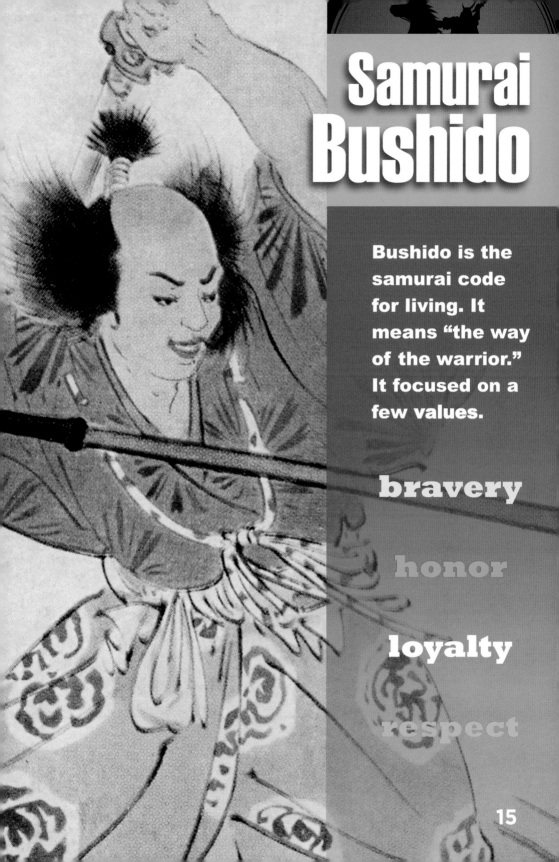

Samurai Bushido

Bushido is the samurai code for living. It means "the way of the warrior." It focused on a few values.

bravery

honor

loyalty

respect

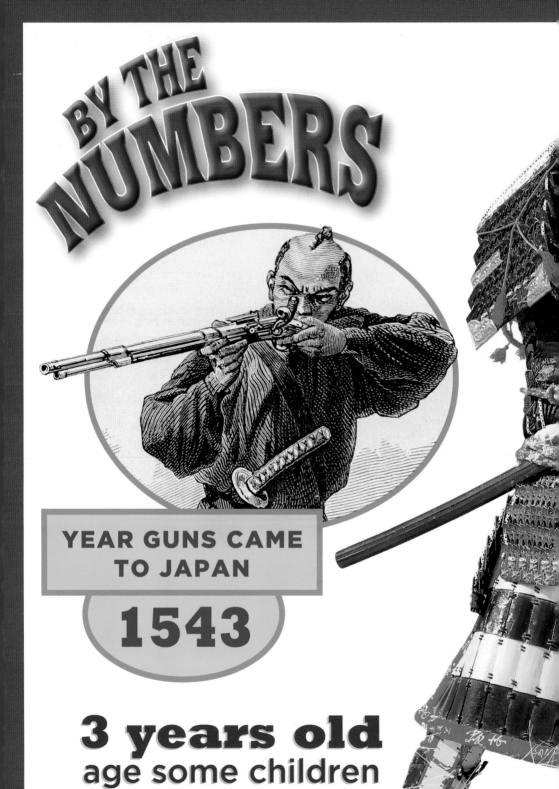

BY THE NUMBERS

YEAR GUNS CAME TO JAPAN

1543

3 years old
age some children began training

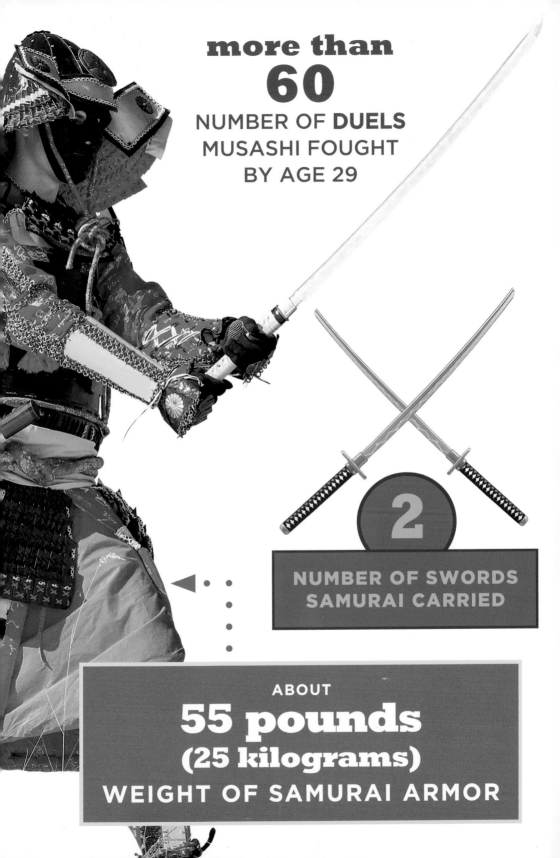

more than
60
NUMBER OF **DUELS**
MUSASHI FOUGHT
BY AGE 29

2
**NUMBER OF SWORDS
SAMURAI CARRIED**

ABOUT
55 pounds
(25 kilograms)
WEIGHT OF SAMURAI ARMOR

Samurai were expected to fight to the death. Some killed themselves if they faced capture or defeat.

Samurai in

Samurai were powerful fighters. They often fought on horses. These warriors are known for their swords. But early samurai fought with bows and arrows. They also used spears with razor-sharp blades. In the 1500s, they began using guns.

Duels, Battles, and Sieges

Samurai fought duels. They also led battles and sieges. During a siege, warriors would surround a castle. They then attacked, blasting the castle with cannons. Or they waited until the people inside ran out of supplies.

In Japan, only samurai were allowed to carry two swords in public.

WEAPONS AND ARMOR

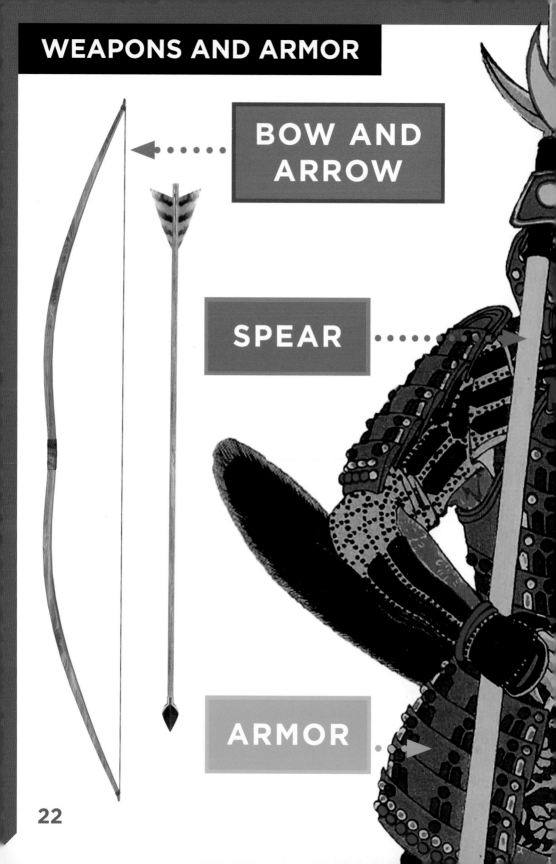

BOW AND ARROW

SPEAR

ARMOR

HELMET

SHORT SWORD

LONG SWORD

23

CHAPTER 4

THE END of the Samurai

In the early 1600s, a time of peace came to Japan. Samurai then took non-fighting roles. Some still served their lords. Others became farmers. But they still followed the way of the warrior.

In the late 1860s, a new ruler came to power. The government then **banned** wearing swords in public. It ended the class system too. The time of the samurai had reached its end.

Samurai Today

Samurai values still exist in Japan. Children learn them at home. Business people use them to make good decisions. People who practice martial arts also use them. • • • • • • • • • • • ▶

Samurai no longer exist. But their beliefs still make a difference today.

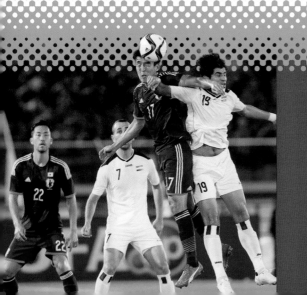

Japan's national soccer team is called Samurai Blue.

TIMELINE

700s
Samurai first start fighting.

1100s
Samurai come to power.

mid-1500s
Samurai begin using guns.

1600s
Japan enters a long
time of peace.

1868
The Meiji
Restoration begins.

ancient (AYN-shunt)—from a time long ago

ban (BAN)—to forbid by law

duel (DOO-uhl)—a fight between two people

honor (AH-ner)—an award or respect for someone

Meiji Restoration (MEY-jee res-tuh-REY-shun)—a political revolution in Japan, starting in 1868, that ended the rule of the shogun; it began the birth of modern Japan.

opponent (uh-POH-nunt)—a person, team, or group that is competing against another

shogun (SHOH-guhn)—any one of the military leaders who ruled Japan until the revolution of 1867–1868

value (VAL-yoo)—a principle or quality that is valuable or desirable

BOOKS

Bodden, Valerie. *Samurai.* Fighters. Mankato, MN: Creative Education / Creative Paperbacks, 2018.

Matthews, Rupert. *Samurai.* History's Fearless Fighters. New York: Gareth Stevens Publishing, 2016.

Nagle, Jeanne. *Samurai.* Warriors around the World. New York: Britannica Educational Publishing, in association with Rosen Educational Services, 2016.

WEBSITES

Japan
kids.nationalgeographic.com/explore/countries/ japan/#japan-gardens.jpg

Japan
kidspast.com/world-history/japan/

Samurai Facts
www.softschools.com/facts/world_history/ samurai_facts/2584/